UK Self-Defence Law
A Practical Guide to Understanding the Law of Defending Yourself

Leigh Simms
LLB (Hons) & 4th Dan Karate

UK Self-Defence Law

A Practical Guide to Understanding the Law of Defending Yourself

Printed in the United Kingdom

First Printed, 2015

Bench Press Publishers
95 Vivian Road
Stoke-on-Trent
Staffordshire
ST4 3JG

Copyright © 2015 Leigh Simms

ISBN: 978-1-326-27517-4

All rights reserved.

This book or any portion thereof may not be reproduced or used in any manner whatsoever without the express written permission of the publisher except for the use of brief quotations in a book review.

Disclaimer: The information in this book is not intended to be used a legal advice and should you have any questions regarding a legal matter you should contact an appropriately qualified professional. The author and publisher accept no liability for any action taken on the basis of the information in this book.

"I think it is the best book on the market on this subject, and it should be a part of your library if you are teaching self-defence or if you are remotely interested in the subject.

Comprehensive and lifesaving."

- Geoff Thompson 8th Dan BCA, WCA

"This short easy to read book is a must for all self-defence and martial arts instructors in England and Wales! A sound understanding of the legalities of self-defence is vital if you are to teach competently. Sadly, what we most frequently see is the law being either completely ignored or misinformation being peddled as if it were fact. This book provides and very easy to understand practical guide that cuts through the misinformation and will be an invaluable resource for teacher and student alike. Leigh Simms has made a superb job of producing this very practical and understandable guide to the legalities of self-defence England and Wales!

All competent and responsible instructors will ensure they read this book."

– Iain Abernethy 6th Dan BCA, WCA

Contents

Acknowledgements xi
Foreword xiii
Introduction 1
Legal Background 5
   Common Law 5
   Statue Law 5
Role of Self-Defence 7
Defining Self-Defence 11
Reasonable Force 15
   Was The Force Reasonable? 15
   Scenario - Defending Yourself 17
Excessive Force 21
Pre-Emptive Striking 25
Mistaking the Facts 29
   Scenario - Mistaking the Facts 29
   Resisting Arrest 30
Duty To Retreat 33
Revenge Attacks 37
Using Weapons in Self-Defence 41
Human Rights & European Law 45
Civil Law 49
Conclusion 53
References 54
   Case Law 55
   Statute Law 55
Statute Law Source Material 57

About the Author

Leigh began martial art training in 1999 under the instruction of Mike Judd 4th Dan Shotokan Karate.

By 2007, Leigh had gained regular success on the competition scene and attained 3 Dan Grades in Shotokan Karate.

Leigh went on to study Practical Karate under Iain Abernethy. In 2011, Leigh achieved his first Dan Grade in Practical Karate.

In 2013, Leigh along side Sensei Mike Judd joined the British Combat Karate Association (BCKA) and both have been certified as registered instructors by Peter Consterdine 9th Dan and Geoff Thompson 8th Dan of the BCKA.

Leigh began studying criminal law and self-defence law during his A-Levels in 2006. In 2008, Leigh continued his study of self-defence law during his Law Degree. After graduating with honours, Leigh furthered his study of self-defence by completing the Post-Graduate Diploma in Legal Practice at the University of Law.

Please visit www.leighsimms.com for more information. Alternatively contact Leigh via email – leigh@leighsimms.com to organise Seminars and Workshops on UK Self-Defence Law.

x

Acknowledgements

First and foremost, I would like to thank my Martial Arts instructor and now close friend Mike Judd for his constant knowledge, support and mentoring he has given me over the last 15 years.

I would also like to thank Iain Abernethy, as his support and guidance over the last couple of years has been invaluable to my own study of martial arts.

Thank you to the many students and training partners that I have crossed paths with over the years.

And finally, thank you to my friends and family for all their help and support as I continue to pursue my martial art and law education.

Foreword

By Geoff Thompson
Author & 8th Dan BCA, WCA

I once appeared on a national radio call-in show as an expert on self-defence. We were talking especially about how important it is to understand the law, in regards to defending yourself in a physical assault. I was dogged in my determination to underline how vital knowledge in this area is, not only for people in the unfortunate position of having to defend themselves in a court of law, post assault, but especially for people teaching self-defence to members of the public.

One exasperated caller wanted to know 'why is this so important?' I told him: 'because people are not convicted in a court of law for what they do in a self-defence situation, they are convicted for what they say in their statement after the fact.'

This is what they are judged on. This information is important. In fact I would say it is imperative if you want to avoid 'the second enemy' the Judiciary.

Many people defend themselves legally, using reasonable force, and are later convicted in court of law, even sent to prison, simply because they did not represent their defence using the right legal jargon.

This amazing book – 20 years overdue – not only tells you how you stand in law regarding your rights to self-defence, but it also offers the correct terminology to use when making a police statement.

I think it is the best book on the market on this subject, and it should be a part of your library if you are teaching self-defence or if you are remotely interested in the subject.

Chapter 1
Introduction

The Law relating to self-defence applies in many different contexts, with its scope covering more than just using force to defend yourself from an attack. Self-Defence can be claimed as a defence if you are:

Defending Other People;

Defending your Property;

Defending your Home; and

Assisting in Prevention of Crime.

Whilst there are many scenarios in which self-defence law can be applied, the primary aim of this e-book is to explain the law in relation to defending yourself should you be a victim of an attack.

Due to the complex and sometimes unclear way the law of self-defence is portrayed in the media, some misconceptions within the law of self-defence have occurred. I hope that by the time you have finished reading this book, some of the misconceptions have been resolved.

For example, one misconception is that, if you have martial art training, you have to warn your attacker about this fact. This is completely false. A person with martial art training is treated the same as an untrained person under the law and does not have to warn their attacker of anything.

Although this book covers UK Law, there are separate laws for Northern Ireland and Scotland. For clarity, any reference in this book to UK Law means the law only in England and Wales.

Self-defence is a legal concept, therefore it is necessary to understand some basic principles of law. Firstly we need to understand the two main ways that laws are created in England and Wales. These being: Common Law and Statute Law.

Chapter 2
Legal Background

Common Law

Common Law (also known as Case Law) is law that is made during a decision by a Legal Judge in a case at Court. A decision made by the Judge is also called a "precedent" as this decision sets a precedent for future cases to follow. Precedents are followed and applied in future cases to ensure that the law remains 'common' throughout the country, hence the term common law.

Statue Law

Statute Law in England & Wales comes in many forms but the main Statutes that relate to self-defence are Acts of Parliament. Whilst there is no need to understand the full process on how an Act is created. However, it is important to understand that they are not made by Judges during legal cases, but instead proposed (usually by political parties) and are debated in the House of Commons and House of Lords as they go through a process of drafting and editing before coming into effect.

Chapter 3
Role of Self-Defence

Self-Defence is a complete legal defence. The defence of self-defence would be claimed if you were arrested and charged with an offence (such as assault & battery, grievous bodily harm or murder), but the reason you acted with physical force was to prevent injury to either yourself or other people. Alternatively, you may be using physical force to protect your property or to assist in the prevention of a crime.

As the general precedent of English Law is "innocent until proven guilty" it is for the prosecution to prove an offence has taken place. As self-defence is a legal defence it would be up to the prosecution to prove to the Jury/Magistrates that you did not act in self-defence or that if you did, then the force used was excessive. This must be proven beyond reasonable doubt for you to be convicted of the accused crime.

A complete defence is a justification for your actions and not an excuse for your actions. If you claim the complete defence of self-defence, you would be pleading "not guilty" to the charge(s) brought against you. To be clear, if you claim self-defence, you are claiming that your actions did not break the law at all.

If the charges make there way to Court, there will be a trial at one of two places, the Magistrates Court or the Crown Court. This would depend on the severity of the charge against you. The Magistrates usually sit as a group of three who judge your case, where at the Crown Court it is a Jury of usually 12 members of the public who decide the outcome your case. It is not necessary for this book to go into full details of this process. But it is important to understand that as self-defence is a complete defence in law, it is an all or nothing claim. This means that there is no middle ground, either:

1. The Magistrates/Jury either find that you acted in self-defence and therefore you committed no crime and you are free to leave the Court; or

2. The Magistrates/Jury find that you did not act in self-defence, therefore you did commit the crime. Then you will be convicted and then sentenced by the Magistrates/Judge.

Furthermore, If you are found guilty of the charge against you then, by default, you did not act in self-defence and would not be able to use it as a reason to be given a lighter sentence.

Chapter 4
Defining Self-Defence

Under common law a person is allowed to use reasonable force to defend himself from an attack, to defend another person from attack and to defend his property. In 1967 an Act of Parliament known as the Criminal Law Act came into force and in addition to the common law definition of self-defence, section 3 of the Criminal Law Act 1976 added the following:

"(1)A person may use such force as is reasonable in the circumstances in the prevention, or in effecting or assisting the lawful arrest of offenders or suspected offenders or of persons unlawfully at large.(2)

Subsection (1) above shall replace the rules of the common law on the question when force used for a purpose mentioned in the subsection is justified by that purpose."

Section 3 of the Criminal Law Act 1967 furthers the scope of self-defence so that it can be used not only in the context of one defending themselves or another, but it also allows self-defence to be used in circumstances where using force can prevent a non-violent crime from taking place.

An example of this would be using force to restrain a shop-lifter, by performing a citizens arrest. In normal circumstances restraining a member of the public would mean that you are committing assault, however if you are restraining them to prevent a crime happening (e.g. to stop them stealing from a shop) or to assist with their arrest (e.g. after they had stole the item), then Section 3 would apply and your actions would be justified under the defence of self-defence.

Chapter 5
Reasonable Force

Both common law and the 1967 Act allude to *reasonable force*. This means that whilst you may use force to defend yourself, there is no defence available if the force is not reasonable. The Court looks at this with the following two stage test:

1. Was the force necessary in the circumstances?
2. Was the force used in a reasonable manner in the circumstances?

Was The Force Reasonable?

The answer to this comes from common law and in particular the case of Palmer 1971, here the judge said the following:

"it will be recognised that a person defending himself cannot weigh to a nicety the exact measure of his necessary defensive action. If a jury thought that in a moment of unexpected anguish a person attacked had only done what he honestly and instinctively

thought was necessary that would be most potent evidence that only reasonable defensive action had been taken."

To summarise, as long as we honestly believe that the force we used in the moment of the attack was necessary, then that is enough to prove that force was necessary, therefore self-defence is available as a defence.

Once force is proven to be necessary, the next question to satisfy is whether the force used was reasonable. Under common law it has been noted that whilst you are judged on the facts as you believe them to be, it is up to the Jury/Magistrates to decide whether or not you acted with reasonable force in those circumstances.

The above questions of necessary and reasonable force have been turned into Statute Law and can now be found in Section's 76(3) and (4) of the Criminal Justice and Immigration Act 2008.

Scenario - Defending Yourself

"You are walking home from work when you notice a stranger walking towards you. He stares at you and then walks directly in your path. You try to move to the side but he moves in front of you again. He shouts at you and grabs your lapel. He punches you in the face and instinctively you hit him back in the jaw, he still holds on to you trying to punch you again but you are able to punch him again and again in the jaw. He falls to the ground holding his jaw and you run home to escape the situation."

Did you act in self-defence? Lets look at the questions that need to be asked. Firstly is there scope for self-defence?

The answer is yes as we have the right to defend ourselves from an attack as stated by Section 3 of the Criminal Law Act 1967. We then look at the two part test for Reasonable Force.

Firstly was the Force Necessary? This is the question of whether you hold an honest belief that force was required in order for you to defend yourself. The answer is yes, as long as you believe that at the moment in time you used force, it was needed.

Stage 2 of the test is whether the force was reasonable? The Jury/Magistrates will decide based on if they believed you acted reasonable in the circumstances as you believed them to be. They will take into the account the fact that you are not likely to be able to calculate the exact amount of force needed due to the nature of being attacked. What the Jury/Magistrates will look for is *whether "in the circumstances you believed them to be, that the level of force you used was reasonable."*

Whilst we can never second guess the Courts decision, in the scenario above, it would seem to be a strong argument that striking the attacker until he was on the ground would be reasonable, given that he was still a threat when he was standing as he had a grip on you and was trying to punch you.

To conclude our scenario, you defended yourself from an attack using force. You believed that using force was necessary and reasonable given the circumstances as you believed them to be.

Chapter 6
Excessive Force

What if, in our scenario, you had decided to stomp on the attackers head three times once he had fallen to the floor? Would it still be self-defence?

Firstly we need to consider if there is scope. Were you defending yourself from an attack? The beginning of the scenario has not changed so the answer would still be yes.

Next we look at the two stage-test. Firstly was force necessary? Here you must have an honest belief that force was necessary. Do you honestly believe it was necessary to stomp the attackers head into the ground three times?

If by somehow you did believe this, the second part of test is for the Jury/Magistrates to decide if the force used was reasonable in the circumstances. In this example, I would believe there is strong evidence to say that it would not be reasonable to continuously stomp on a persons head once they are on the ground and no longer a threat.

Sometimes this two-part test can seem a little confusing, but when it relates to excessive force, I hope you can see its importance and why it is necessary to have the first question as "is force necessary" - which is subjective (i.e. based on what you believe the circumstances to be) and the second question - "was the force reasonable?" - which is objective (i.e. based on what the reasonable person would do in the circumstances).

This two stage test acts a safeguard to prevent people who claim self-defence after legitimately defending themselves but then deciding to go further and use further force to assault/murder their attack when they were no longer in immediate danger of being harmed.

Chapter 7
Pre-Emptive Striking

But if you believed, because of the attackers actions, that harm was about to be caused to you and you made a decision to hit the attacker first, to prevent him from physically attacking you. Are you actions still classed as self-defence?

There is nothing in law that states you have to wait to be attacked, in fact the law clearly states the opposite is true and that you don't have to wait to be struck first before you strike back. In the case of Beckford 1988, Lord Griffiths said

"a man about to be attacked does not have to wait for his assailant to strike the first blow or fire the first shot; circumstances may justify a pre-emptive strike."

Using a pre-emptive strike is completely legal in terms of self-defence as long as you believe you were in immediate danger and that force was necessary.

Chapter 8
Mistaking the Facts

Scenario - Mistaking the Facts

You witnessed a man physically attack a woman, so you rush to her aid and attack the man. But in fact, the lady had just committed a theft and the man had tackled her to the ground to stop her from escaping. Can you claim you acted in self-defence of the lady by attacking the man?

The scenario above is very similar to the real life case of R v Gladstone Williams 1984. The ruling stated that if you make a mistake on the facts of the situation, then you will be judged on whether the force you used was reasonable for the facts you believed. Remember, you are judged on the facts as you believe them to be. Therefore, it is enough for your to rely on your belief in what you thought happened, even though the actual facts show that the man was using force lawfully and he was committing no crime against her.

Also, it does not matter why you made the mistake or even how reasonable the mistake you made is (as stated in the case of Morgan 1976). This is now contained in subsection 4 of section76 CJIA 2008 as well as case law. However, if you hold a mistaken belief because being voluntarily intoxicated (e.g. under the influence of alcohol or drugs) then you will not be able to rely on self-defence. Subsection 5 of section 76 CJIA 2008 covers this point.

Resisting Arrest
This also extends to resisting arrest scenarios. If you did not believe you were being arrested and used force to resist the arrest, then you can still claim self-defence, assuming the force you used was reasonable.

However, it is not possible to claim self-defence if you knew you were about to be be arrested and decide to resist because you have not committed the offence you are being arrested on suspicion of committing.

There are different rules in relation to making a mistake as to the facts in respect to Civil Law. This will be dealt with at Chapter 13.

Chapter 9
Duty To Retreat

Is it still possible to claim self-defence when you use force to defend yourself, even if you had the option to retreat and walk away from the confrontation?

The first issue raised is whether you can consent to your own assault. Besides a few exceptions, you cannot agree to your own assault, however, even though you don't agree to being assaulted, it does not necessarily mean you acted in self-defence. It could be that you intended to fight the other person, in which case you would be committing a crime too. Therefore the question is whether deciding not to retreat still allows the defence of self-defence to be used.

Interestingly, under common law you do not have to retreat, nor do you have to show an unwillingness to fight in order to use the defence of self-defence. This was established in the case of Bird 1985. However, the fact that you did not retreat will more than likely be a factor to be taken into consideration by the Jury/Magistrates who decide the verdict of the case.

It is also possible not to back-down and use a pre-emptive strike as long as you believed you were in immediate unlawful danger at the time and that force used was reasonable.

Chapter 10
Revenge Attacks

What is the law if you decide to extract revenge on your enemy for something they have done to you in the past? If you arrived at the location of your enemy and a physical fight breaks out. Are you able to claim self-defence?

In the case of Rashford 2005, the Judge noted that just because the defendant went somewhere to exact revenge, it does not necessarily rule out self-defence as a defence.

Even though in Rashford it was not ruled out that self-defence could be used a defence, it is worth noting that if you intended to be the aggressor in the situation and began the fight, you could not claim self-defence when the other party attacked you back and you used force to defend those attacks. The law understands that during the course of a fight you will try at times to defend yourself from the other person involved. However, if you volunteered into the fight then your actions are not lawful and cannot be considered self-defence.

Chapter 11
Using Weapons in Self-Defence

Before looking at the use of weapons in a self-defence situation, it is important to understand the general weapon laws in the UK. Under the Prevention of Crime Act 1953, it is illegal to have in your possession an offensive weapon without a lawful reason or excuse. An offensive weapon is defined as: *"any article made or adapted for use to causing injury to the person, or intended by the person having it with him for such use."* Additionally in the case of Simpson, the Judge identified three different categories of offensive weapons. These are as follows:

Those made for causing injury to the person;
Those adapted for such a purpose; and
Those not so made or adapted, but carried with the intention of causing injury to the person.

If the weapon was carried with "lawful authority or reasonable excuse" then no offence by law has been committed.

In relation to knives and other pointed weapons, Section 139 of the Criminal Justice Act 1988 makes it illegal for you to have a blade or other sharply pointed item that has a cutting edge of over 3 inches with you in public.

In addition to the defence of *"lawful authority or reasonable excuse"*, there are a further three lawful defences available for carrying a blade with a cutting edge of over 3 inches. These defences make it lawful to carry the blade if it is:

For use at work; or

With the person for religious reasons; or

With the person as part of a national costume.

Please note that in relation to both Offensive Weapons as defined in the Prevention of Crime Act and the Criminal Justice Act, there is no such defence for carrying a weapon for use in self-defence situations. Nor does the law classify certain weapons as *self-defence weapons*. However, assuming you use reasonable force, you are allowed to defend yourself by using ordinary everyday objects (for example; keys or umbrella) as long as they were carried for their everyday purpose.

Chapter 12
Human Rights & European Law

The Human Rights Act and the European Convention on Human Rights also govern the law in the UK. In Article 2 of the Convention it states that:

1. Everyone's right to life shall be protected by law. No one shall be deprived of his life intentionally save in the execution of a sentence of a court following his conviction of a crime for which this penalty is provided by law.

2. Deprivation of life shall not be regarded as inflicted in contravention of this article when it results from the use of force which is no more than absolutely necessary:

(a) in defence of any person from unlawful violence;

(b) in order to effect a lawful arrest or to prevent escape of a person lawfully detained;

(c) in action lawfully taken for the purpose of quelling a riot or insurrection.

This means that if you are attacked and you use reasonable force to defend yourself and the attacker is killed as a result then the "right to life" under Article 2 is not breached because the attacker's initial attack on you would have removed their right. However, if you use excessive force on the attacker then "right to life" under Article 2 may have been broken.

One of the key differences between European Law and UK Law is that under UK Law, self-defence is an option as a defence, if you hold an honest belief that force is necessary, even if based on the facts, force was not actually necessary. However, under Article 2 of the Convention such mistakes of the facts must be both reasonable and objectively assessed by the Court.

Whether or not this distinction is relevant in practice is not clear. In the 2007 case of R (Bennett) the Judge said:

"the European Court of Human Rights has considered what English law requires for self defence, and has not suggested that there is any incompatibility with Article 2."

This seems to suggest that killing someone in self-defence under UK law will not cause a breach of Article 2 on the European Convention of Human Rights.

Chapter 13
Civil Law

As well as being a defence for criminal charges, self-defence can also be claimed if you are being sued for assault in the Civil Courts. Whilst it is rare for civil charges to be brought in a situation where you are being accused of attacking someone, it is still a possibility.

The defence of self-defence applies with the same rules except a small exception. In the case of Ashley, the Judged states as follows:

"It is one thing to say that if A's mistaken belief was honestly held he should not be punished by the criminal law. It would be quite another to say that A's unreasonably held mistaken belief would be sufficient to justify the law in setting aside B's right not to be subjected to physical violence by A. I would have no hesitation whatever in holding that for civil law purposes an excuse of self defence based on non-existent facts that are honestly but unreasonably believed to exist must fail."

To summarise, the ruling stated that it would not be right in the civil courts to claim self-defence if you made a mistake of the facts of the circumstances that were unreasonable to make. This is in contrast with the criminal case law that allows a mistake on the facts as long as you held an honest belief of those facts.

In reality, the kind of scenarios that would cause a civil claim against you are incredibly slim. Especially when it relates to the scenario of defending yourself from an attack. A scenario that is more applicable is, if person A uses force on an innocent person B, because of As belief that B was about to commit a crime. If As belief was unreasonable but honestly held, then under criminal law A can claim self-defence. Under civil law B has grounds to sue A for compensation as he was assaulted because of As unreasonable belief. To ensure compliance with both criminal and civil law, it is good practice to ensure your beliefs of the facts are both honestly and reasonably held.

Chapter 14
Conclusion

In essence, the law of England & Wales takes a very common sense approach to dealing with self-defence. In reality it comes down to three questions -

1. Is there Scope for self-defence to be applied?
2. If yes, did you believe force was necessary due to the circumstances?
3. If yes, was the amount of force used reasonable given the circumstances?

If all three of the above questions can be answered yes, then self-defence can be relied upon. For a clear quote that summarised self-defence we can look at the ruling in the case of Balogun 1999:

"a man who is attacked or believes that he is about to be attacked may use such force as is both necessary and reasonable in order to defend himself. If that is what he does then he acts lawfully."

Chapter 4
Conclusion

References

Case Law

Mistaken Facts – Morgan [1976] AC 182

Mistake & Involuntary Intoxication – O' Grady [1987] QB 995

Mistaken Facts - Williams (Gladstone) [1987] 78 Cr App R 276

Pre-Emptive Striking – Beckford [1988] 1 AC 130

Preventing an attack on another person – Rose [1884] 15 Cox 540

Reasonable Force – Palmer [1971] AC 814

Retreating – Bird [1985] 1 WLR 816

Revenge - R v Rashford [2005] EWCA Crim 3377

Self-Defence & Civil Law – Ashley (Fc) and Another (Fc) V Chief Constable of Sussex Police [2008] UKHL 25

Self-Defence & The European Convention on Human Rights - R (Bennett) v HM Coroner for Inner London [2007] EWCA Civ 617

Statute Law

Blades & Pointed Weapons – Section 139 Criminal Justice Act 1988

Definition of Self-Defence - Section 3 Criminal Law Act 1967

Human Rights Law –Article 2 of the European Convention on Human Rights

Mistaken Facts – Section 76(5) Criminal Justice and Immigration Act 2008

Offensive Weapons – Prevention of Crime Act 1953

Reasonable Force – Section 76(3) & (4) Criminal Justice and Immigration Act 2008

Statute Law Source Material

The following material is presented for those readers who wish to see the full sections of Statute Law in their entirety. The information below is subject to Crown Copyright and is being reproduced with the permission of the Controller of HMSO and the Queen's Printer for Scotland.

Definition of Self-Defence - Section 3 Criminal Law Act 1967
3. Use of force in making arrest, etc.

(1) A person may use such force as is reasonable in the circumstances in the prevention of crime, or in effecting or assisting in the lawful arrest of offenders or suspected offenders or of persons unlawfully at large.

(2) Subsection (1) above shall replace the rules of the common law on the question when force used for a purpose mentioned in the subsection is justified by that purpose.

Blades & Pointed Weapons – Section 139 Criminal Justice Act 1988

139. Offence of having article with blade or point in public place.

(1)Subject to subsections (4) and (5) below, any person who has an article to which this section applies with him in a public place shall be guilty of an offence.

(2)Subject to subsection (3) below, this section applies to any article which has a blade or is sharply pointed except a folding pocketknife.

(3)This section applies to a folding pocketknife if the cutting edge of its blade exceeds 3 inches.

(4)It shall be a defence for a person charged with an offence under this section to prove that he had good reason or lawful authority for having the article with him in a public place.

(5)Without prejudice to the generality of subsection (4) above, it shall be a defence for a person charged with an offence under this section to prove that he had the article with him—

(a)for use at work;

(b)for religious reasons; or

(c)as part of any national costume.

(6)A person guilty of an offence under subsection (1) above shall be liable-

(a)on summary conviction, to imprisonment for a term not exceeding six months, or a fine not exceeding the statutory maximum, or both;

(b)on conviction on indictment, to imprisonment for a term not exceeding four years, or a fine, or both.

(7)In this section "public place" includes any place to which at the material time the public have or are permitted access, whether on payment or otherwise.

(8)This section shall not have effect in relation to anything done before it comes into force.

Offensive Weapons – Prevention of Crime Act 1953

1. Prohibition of the carrying of offensive weapons without lawful authority or reasonable excuse.

(1)Any person who without lawful authority or reasonable excuse, the proof whereof shall lie on him, has with him in any public place any offensive weapon shall be guilty of an offence, and shall be liable—

(a)on summary conviction, to imprisonment for a term not exceeding six months or a fine not exceeding £200, or both;

(b)on conviction on indictment, to imprisonment for a term not exceeding four years or a fine not exceeding one hundred pounds, or both.

(2)Where any person is convicted of an offence under subsection (1) of this section the court may make an order for the forfeiture or disposal of any weapon in respect of which the offence was committed.

3)A constable may arrest without warrant any person whom he has reasonable cause to believe to be committing an offence under subsection (1) of this section, if the constable is not satisfied as to that person's identity or place of residence, or has reasonable cause to believe that it is necessary to arrest him in order to prevent the commission by him of any other offence in the course of committing which an offensive weapon might be used.

(4)In this section "public place" includes any highway, or in Scotland any road within the meaning of the Roads (Scotland) Act 1984 and any other premises or place to which at the material time the public have or are permitted to have access, whether on payment or otherwise; and "offensive weapon" means any article made or adapted for use for causing injury to the person, or intended by the person having it with him for such use by him or by some other person.

2. Short title, commencement and extent

(1)This Act may be cited as the Prevention of Crime Act 1953.

(2)This Act shall come into operation on the expiration of one month from the passing thereof.

(3)This Act shall not extend to Northern Ireland.

Mistaken Facts & Reasonable Force – Section 76 Criminal Justice and Immigration Act 2008

76. Reasonable force for purposes of self-defence etc.

(1)This section applies where in proceedings for an offence—

(a)an issue arises as to whether a person charged with the offence ("D") is entitled to rely on a defence within subsection (2), and

(b)the question arises whether the degree of force used by D against a person ("V") was reasonable in the circumstances.

(2)The defences are—

(a)the common law defence of self-defence; and

(b)the defences provided by section 3(1) of the Criminal Law Act 1967 (c. 58) or section 3(1) of the Criminal Law Act (Northern Ireland) 1967 (c. 18 (N.I.)) (use of force in prevention of crime or making arrest).

(3)The question whether the degree of force used by D was reasonable in the circumstances is to be decided by reference to the circumstances as D believed them to be, and subsections (4) to (8) also apply in connection with deciding that question.

(4)If D claims to have held a particular belief as regards the existence of any circumstances—

(a)the reasonableness or otherwise of that belief is relevant to the question whether D genuinely held it; but

(b)if it is determined that D did genuinely hold it, D is entitled to rely on it for the purposes of subsection (3), whether or not—

(i)it was mistaken, or

(ii)(if it was mistaken) the mistake was a reasonable one to have made.

(5)But subsection (4)(b) does not enable D to rely on any mistaken belief attributable to intoxication that was voluntarily induced.

(6)The degree of force used by D is not to be regarded as having been reasonable in the circumstances as D believed them to be if it was disproportionate in those circumstances.

(7)In deciding the question mentioned in subsection (3) the following considerations are to be taken into account (so far as relevant in the circumstances of the case)—

(a)that a person acting for a legitimate purpose may not be able to weigh to a nicety the exact measure of any necessary action; and

(b)that evidence of a person's having only done what the person honestly and instinctively thought was necessary for a legitimate purpose constitutes strong evidence that only reasonable action was taken by that person for that purpose.

(8)Subsection (7) is not to be read as preventing other matters from being taken into account where they are relevant to deciding the question mentioned in subsection (3).

(9)This section is intended to clarify the operation of the existing defences mentioned in subsection (2).

(10)In this section—

(a)"legitimate purpose" means—

>(i)the purpose of self-defence under the common law, or

>(ii)the prevention of crime or effecting or assisting in the lawful arrest of persons mentioned in the provisions referred to in subsection (2)(b);

(b)references to self-defence include acting in defence of another person; and

(c)references to the degree of force used are to the type and amount of force used.

More from the Author

UK Self-Defence Law 2:
A Practical Guide to Understanding the Law of Defending Your Property

"Defending your home from intruders has become a highly controversial area of law largely due to the media and the famous case of Tony Martin from the 1990s. In this book Leigh dispels the myths and misconceptions surrounding self-defence in the home by breaking down the legal rules into clear and simple language that is easy for everyone to understand."

Visit www.leighsimms.com for more information on how to claim your free copy of the above book and to receive up-to-date information on the release of UK Self-Defence Law 3: Legal Self-Defence Training Drills for Martial Artists.

Coming Soon:
UK Self-Defence Law 3: Legal Self-Defence Training Drills for Martial Artists

Seminars & Workshops
If you would like to host Leigh for a seminar or workshop please contact info@leighsimms.com or call 07581443637.